Native Americans

Eastern Woodlands Indians

Mir Tamim Ansary

Heinemann Library
Chicago, Illinois

© 2000 Reed Educational & Professional Publishing
Published by Heinemann Library,
an imprint of Reed Educational & Professional Publishing,
100 N. LaSalle, Suite 1010
Chicago, IL 60602

Customer Service 888-454-2279

Printed in Hong Kong
Designed by Depke Design

04 03 02 01 00
10 9 8 7 6 5 4 3 2 1

Library of Congress Cataloging-in-Publication Data
Ansary, Mir Tamim.
     Eastern woodlands Indians / Mir Tamim Ansary.
         p. cm. – (Native Americans)
     Includes bibliographical references and index.
     Summary: Introduces the history, dwellings, artwork, religious
beliefs, clothing, food, and other elements of life of the Native
American peoples of the eastern woodlands of North America.
     ISBN 1-57572-930-X (library binding)
     1. Woodland Indians-Juvenile literature. 2. Iroquois Indians
–Juvenile literature. 3. Algonquian Indians-Juvenile literature.
[1. Indians of North America-Canada, Eastern. 2. Indians of North
America-East (U.S.)] I Title. II. Series: Ansary, Mir Tamim.
Native Americans.
E78.E2A59 2000
973'.04973-dc21

                                                    99-34900
                                                       CIP

Acknowledgments
The author and publishers are grateful to the following for permission to reproduce copyright material:
Cover photograph· The Granger Collection
The Bridgeman Art Library, p. 14 top; Corbis/Bettmann-UPI pp. 24, 29; Dr. E.R. Degginger, pp. 5, 28; Phil Degginger,
p. 16; The Granger Collection, pp. 7, 8, 9, 10, 12, 14, 15, 19, 20, 21, 23, 25, 26, 30; Ben Klaffke, p. 11; National
Geographic Image Collection/Kenneth Love, p. 18; Northwind Pictures, pp. 13, 17, 22, 27; Stock Montage, Inc., p. 30 top.

Every effort has been made to contact copyright holders of any material reproduced in this book. Any omissions will be
rectified in subsequent printings if notice is given to the publisher.

Our special thanks to Lana Grant, Native American MLS, for her
help in the preparation of this book.

Note to the Reader Some words are shown in bold, **like this.** You can find
out what they mean by looking in the glossary.

Contents

The Eastern Woodlands 4

Algonquin and Iroquois 6

Farming, Hunting, and Fishing 8

Beautiful Clothing 10

Longhouse and Wigwam 12

Wampum and Tobacco 14

The Spirit World 16

Festivals and Ceremonies 18

Groups of Tribes 20

Europeans Arrive 22

The Wars 24

Losing the Land 26

The 20th Century 28

Famous Eastern Woodlands Indians . . 30

Glossary *31*

More Books to Read *32*

Index *32*

The Eastern Woodlands

The Eastern Woodlands region stretches from the Great Lakes to the Atlantic Ocean. The St. Lawrence River connects these lakes to the ocean. Smaller lakes dot the region as well. Several other large rivers wind through it. And from Virginia to northern Canada, the Atlantic coast has good natural harbors.

Long ago, thick woods covered this whole region. They were mostly broadleaf trees—the kind that lose their leaves in the fall. Birch, elm, and oak were common. Cedar trees grew here, too. The woods stretched north into present-day Canada. They stretched south to the Ohio River valley and beyond.

Algonquin and Iroquois

People first came to this region about 9,000 years ago. They were hunters. They probably spoke early forms of a language called *Algonquin*. Some of their **descendants** settled along the Atlantic Coast. Others, such as the Ojibwa, ended up near the Great Lakes.

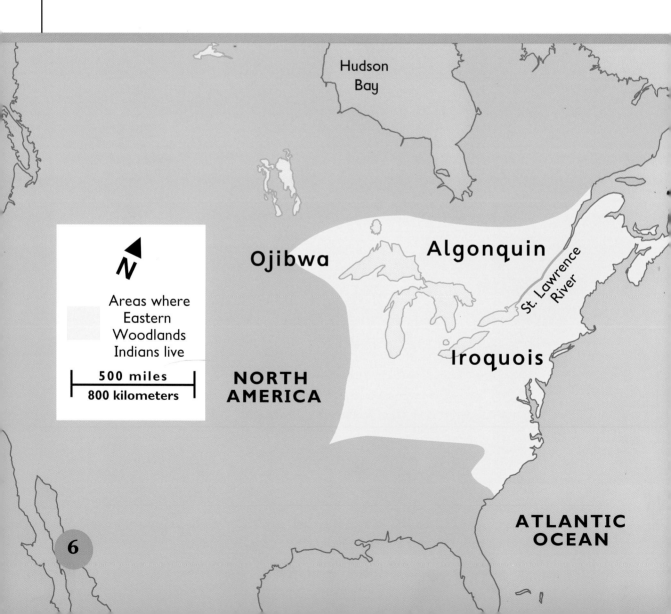

Hudson Bay

N

Areas where Eastern Woodlands Indians live

500 miles
800 kilometers

Ojibwa

Algonquin

St. Lawrence River

Iroquois

NORTH AMERICA

ATLANTIC OCEAN

About 3,000 years ago, a new **culture** began here.
It was centered near modern-day Hopewell, Ohio.
These people were farmers. They probably spoke
an Iroquoian language. They built huge mounds
as graves for their leaders. Their ways spread far. By
1500, many powerful Iroquois tribes lived along the
St. Lawrence River.

*The Hopewell people made mounds that
looked like animals. This "snake" in Ohio is
more than 1,300 feet (396 meters) long.*

Farming, Hunting, and Fishing

For the native people of the Eastern Woodlands, summer and fall were farming seasons. They grew 17 kinds of corn, 60 kinds of beans, and at least 7 types of squash. They also gathered wild rice and other plants for food and medicine. The Ojibwa used sap from maple trees to make candies and drinks.

These Iroquois women are grinding corn or dried berries, while a papoose, or baby, naps.

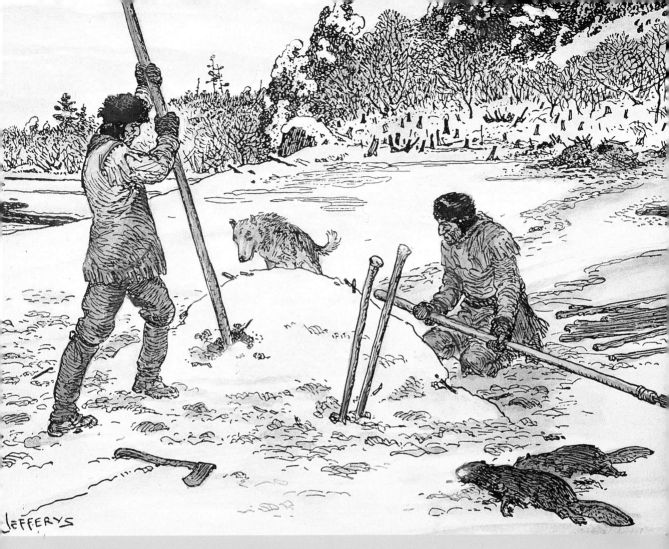

Corn was planted in small hills. Once it sprouted, beans were planted in the same hill.

After the harvest, many Eastern Woodlands villages emptied out. Families went hunting for the winter. They hunted beaver, otter, muskrat, deer, and other animals. Spring brought the fishing season. The northern lakes were often still frozen. But the Indians cut holes in the ice and fished through the holes.

Beautiful Clothing

Hunters were interested in skins, feathers, and bones as well as meat. The early Indians of this region made their clothes from **buckskin** and other types of leather. Later, they started using cloth they got from European traders. Women wore long dresses. Men usually wore leggings, **kilts**, and caps with feathers.

Men and women wore jewelry made of bone, hair, copper, colorful stones, feathers, and shells.

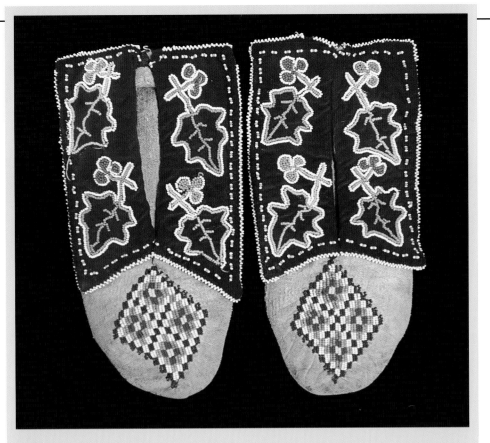

These flowerlike patterns became popular among the Iroquois after they started trading with Europeans.

Clothes were decorated with dyes, beads, **quills**, and moose hair. Indians made beads from natural items such as shells and teeth. But later they got glass beads from European traders. Their art styles changed at this point. The Iroquois, for example, began using curved lines and flowerlike patterns.

Longhouse and Wigwam

The Iroquois lived in "longhouses." A longhouse was about 65 feet (20 meters) long and 18 feet (6 meters) wide. Up to 20 families lived in each longhouse. Family members were related through their mothers—they belonged to the same **clan**. Each village had many clans. Each clan had houses in many villages. Women were leaders of the clans.

Many clans usually lived in an Iroquois village, each in its own longhouse.

12

Sheets of bark placed over this frame will make the walls of this wigwam.

Most Algonquin tribes built wigwams, which were smaller houses made of poles and bark. Tribes along the sea lived in settled villages. They made sturdy dome-shaped wigwams. Those near the Great Lakes were **nomads**. They lived in smaller cone-shaped wigwams that could be built quickly, or rebuilt using frames from the year before.

Wampum and Tobacco

Both Iroquois and Algonquin tribes made wampum. This was a beaded belt of colored shells. The pattern of the shells had a meaning. Wampum often tells the story of a great event. Leaders traded wampum to make agreements. Eventually, wampum was traded for goods, much like money.

The beads in this belt of wampum are made of small shells with holes drilled in them.

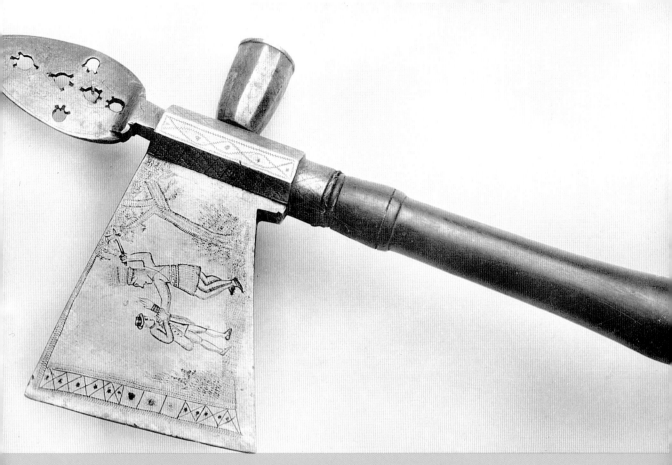

In the Eastern Woodlands, a messenger would carry a pipe like this to show that he came to talk—not fight.

Tobacco, too, was used to seal important promises. For example, when two tribes made peace, the leaders smoked a special "peace pipe" together. Tobacco was used because it was seen as a **sacred** plant. The Indians believed its smoke connected a person's prayers to the world of **spirits**.

The Spirit World

The Native Americans of the Eastern Woodlands had strong religious beliefs. These ideas are still very important. They teach that everything in nature has a **spirit**. The Three Sisters, for example, are the spirits of corn, beans, and squash. All life, including spirits, have been created by one Great Spirit.

To the Native Americans of the Eastern Woodlands, a plant like this has its own spirit.

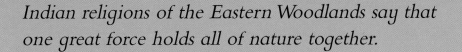

Indian religions of the Eastern Woodlands say that one great force holds all of nature together.

The Great Spirit in Indian religions is a force that is in everything and that is everywhere. This force weaves the world together. The Iroquois called it *orenda*. The Algonquins called it *manitou*. When Indians spoke of "medicine," they meant a connection to this force.

Festivals and Ceremonies

Indian life was rich with celebrations. Many religious festivals were about crops. The Iroquois, for example, celebrated the planting and the harvest. When the green corn got ripe, they had a festival. They had another for blueberries, and so on. The Algonquin tribes had similar festivals.

This young Chippewa is dancing at a harvest festival in traditional clothing.

Masks like this were supposed to scare away evil spirits.

Not all **ceremonies** were about having fun, however. One Iroquois group was called the False Face Society. The members wore ugly masks cut from living trees. At certain times in spring and fall, they went from house to house. They did this to scare away ghosts and evil **spirits**.

Groups of Tribes

Tribes often joined together into larger groups called nations or **confederacies.** Four powerful tribes around Lake Huron formed the Huron Confederacy. Another Algonquin group was called the Tobacco Nation. Two hundred villages near Chesapeake Bay belonged to the Powhattan Confederacy. The most powerful confederacy was the Iroquois League, which was started around 1570.

Leaders of five tribes gather to work out laws for the new Iroquois League.

20

The Iroquois League included the Mohawk, Seneca, Onondaga, Cayuga, and Oneida tribes. The Tuscarora joined later. Fifty sachems, or chiefs, from these tribes met each year for a Great Council. High-ranking women of their **clans** chose them. These sachems made laws, settled arguments, and decided matters of peace and war.

Europeans Arrive

In the 16th century, Europeans began exploring North America. They brought tools, guns, glassware, beads, and cloth to America. The Indians traded furs to get the European goods. Tribes were soon killing more animals than ever to get trade goods. In some areas, many of the animals with fur were killed.

European traders got rich on furs they bought from the Indians of the Eastern Woodlands.

Europeans made over 500 voyages to the Eastern Woodlands by 1620, often bringing deadly diseases to this land.

Many tribes then started fighting to control lands and the waterways that the animals needed to survive. The Indians needed the furs to keep trading with the Europeans. However, the Europeans also brought illness and diseases with them. Some European illnesses were deadly to Indians. These illnesses spread fast and far. Whole villages of Indians died before even meeting Europeans.

The Wars

In 1649, the Iroquois League, or group, destroyed the Huron **Confederacy**. They went on to destroy all the Hurons' **allies**. Survivors of these battles fled in all directions. But wherever they tried to settle, they had to fight the tribes already living there. The whole Eastern Woodlands became an area of war.

War in the Eastern Woodlands drove many tribes out of the woods and onto the western prairie.

The French and Indian War was really a war between the French and the British. The Indians took sides.

The Europeans were at war, too. Beginning in 1689, the French fought the British for control of North America. The Indians took sides in many of these battles. Finally, in 1763, the British defeated the French and drove them almost completely out of North America. Then the British turned on the Indians, including their former allies.

Losing the Land

Pontiac, an Ottawa chieftain, tried to **unite** the Indians against all Whites. In 1763, his forces took over the Ohio Valley. But when summer ended, the Indian warriors went home. It was not the Indian way to make war year round. So the British took back what they had lost. Pontiac's dream died.

Pontiac united sixteen major tribes against the British, but he could not hold his warriors together.

Indian tribes of the Eastern Woodlands were forced or tricked into signing treaties that took away their lands from them.

Most tribes sided with the British in the American Revolution. Afterwards, they faced new hardships. George Washington gave their lands to his American soldiers. Some Iroquois moved to Canada. Other Indians were forced onto small **reservations**. By 1880, Whites had taken over almost all Indian land in the Eastern Woodlands.

The 20th Century

Over half the Native Americans of the Eastern Woodlands now live in cities. In fact, they have helped to build those cities. Mohawk construction workers are fearless about working high above ground. So they have done much of the work on the tall buildings of East Coast cities, such as New York.

Mohawk construction workers have helped build many bridges and buildings in the east.

At this Grand Council of the American Indian, leaders from several tribes plan a course for Native Americans in the modern world.

The Indian past is on display at places like the Oneida Nation Museum in Green Bay, Wisconsin. But Indian ways are still alive on **reservations** from Minnesota to Pennsylvania. The Iroquois League still exists, for example. The Great Council still meets once a year to plan a future for today's Iroquois.

Famous Eastern Woodlands Indians

Ely Samuel Parker (Seneca, 1828–1895) became a sachem of his tribe at 23. But he also studied law and engineering at White schools. During the Civil War, he became General Grant's chief assistant. Later, when Grant became U.S. president, Parker was appointed Commissioner of Indian Affairs.

Tecumseh (Shawnee, 1768–1813) was a war chief of the Shawnee nation. He dreamed of **uniting** all Indian tribes and building one great Indian nation. In 1812, his powerful army captured Detroit. But William Harrison defeated and killed Tecumseh in 1813 at the Battle of Tippecanoe.

Bill Miller (Mohican, 1955–) is a musician. His band has played with Pearl Jam and toured with Tori Amos. He writes poetry, sings, and plays the flute. His albums include *Raven In The Snow* and *The Red Road*. He is an artist too: his paintings appear on many CD covers.

Glossary

allies people or groups who are on the same side in a fight or struggle

buckskin soft leather made from deerskin

ceremony set of acts that have special meaning, often for religious reasons

clan group of families that shares an ancestor

confederacy people or groups working together toward the same goals

culture special way of life of a group of people, including their ideas, skills, arts, and tools they use

descendant person who is born of someone—children, grandchildren, and so on down through time.

kilt kneelength skirt, often worn by a man

nomad person who moves from place to place without a home, usually moving to be near better food sources

quill sharp, thornlike part growing from animals' skin

reservation lands set aside specially for Native Americans

sacred worthy of respect for religious reasons

spirit being that has life but cannot be seen, often having special powers

unite join into one group

More Books to Read

Duvall, Jill D. *The Seneca.* Danbury, Conn: Children's Press, 1991.

Lund, Bill. *The Iroquois Indians.* Danbury, Conn: Children's Press, 1997.

Wheeler, Jill. *The Story of Pontiac.* Minneapolis, Minn: ABDO Publishing Company, 1989.

Index

Algonquin 6, 13, 14, 17, 18, 20
American Revolution 27

Cayuga 21
Chesapeake Bay 20
clan 12, 21
clothing 10, 11, 18

Detroit, Michigan 30

False Face Society 19
farming 7, 8, 9
French 25
Fur Trade 22

Great Council 21, 29
Great Lakes 4, 6, 13
Great Spirit 16, 17

Harrison, William 30
harvest 9, 18
Hopewell, Ohio 7
Huron Confederacy 20, 24

Iroquois 6, 7, 11, 12, 14, 17
Iroquois League 20, 21, 24

medicine 8, 17, 29
Miller, Bill 30
Mohawk 21, 28
Mohican 30
money 14

Ohio River 5
Ojibwa 6, 8
Oneida 21. 29

Oneida Nation Museum 29
Onondaga 21
Ottawa 26

Parker, Ely Samuel 30
Pontiac 26
Powhattan Confederacy 20

sachems 21
Seneca 21, 30
Shawnee 30
spirits 15, 16, 17, 19

Tecumseh 30
Tuscarora 21

wampum 14
Washington, George 27